W9-CTM-276

FLY LEADERS & KNOTS

Written and Illustrated by
Larry V. Notley

Published in 1998 by **Frank Amato Publications, Inc.**
P.O. Box 82112, Portland, Oregon 97282
(503) 653-8108

ISBN: 1-57188-122-2
UPC: 0-66066-00319-5
Cover Photo: Tony Amato
All Drawings: Larry Notley
Layout: Ann Amato
Printed in Canada.

10 9 8 7 6 5 4 3 2

Table of Contents

Introduction

This book is to be used as a reference and technical guide for the construction of leaders and the pertinent aspects of constructing said leaders. I like to think that I know what fly fishermen want in the way of technical information, so let's cut to the chase. This is a technical book about knots and the various leaders you'll need to catch a wide variety of fish. You should then be able to catch the fish you want, have a great trip, and send me your stories. Isn't that what it is really all about, what you did, and what the next person can do?

I am technically minded. I have 18 years experience in the engineering field as a designer and manager, and 10 years experience in the printing business as vice-president of sales and marketing. I've been fly fishing since 1976 and presently, I am the owner and operator of my own fly fishing manufacturing, distributing, and retail company. These trades I do know. So, with my above-mentioned skills, I finally decided to put my notes and experience to work. This combination led to the creation of this working manual of leaders, knots, and information.

When I first started fly fishing, I needed a leader for bass. So off to the local dealer I went. As my experience increased and communications with others progressed, I wanted to tie my own leaders. This became a feat—where to go, what to read, or who to ask.

Have you ever tried to remember in which magazine you saw a particular leader? Or, to remember one that was shared with you? As you know, you'll go nuts trying to remember where you saw or heard about a particular leader. So, over the past 15 years I have collected drawings, sketches, and working notes, and put them together, resulting in this book.

I found myself hunting through mounds of folders containing notes to find information on workable leaders for specific needs. It was inevitable that one day I would mesh all of this information together and write this book.

After starting my fly fishing business, Pockit Sports Co., customers would call, or write, inquiring about leaders and necessary knots they would need for the type of fishing they were going to do. My response is this handy compact book that will address those needs.

I hope you enjoy this book as much as I enjoyed putting it together, and I hope you find what you need. If you have a special leader that you would like to share, please feel free to send me the specifications, and a working leader.

Thank you and happy fishing,

Larry V. Notley
Galactic Warlord and Mad Dog Fly Fisher

Section One
General Information

Leader/Tippet to Hook Size

The following measurements are in standard inches with the breaking strength in pounds. (Each can vary from manufacturer to manufacturer.)

Tippet Size	Diameter (Inches)	Pound Test	Fly or Hook Size
0X	.011	15 lb.	2 - 1/0
1X	.010	12 lb.	1 - 6
2X	.009	9.5 lb.	2 - 8
3X	.008	8.0 lb.	4 - 10
4X	.007	6.5 lb.	6 - 12
5X	.006	5.5 lb.	8 - 14
6X	.005	3.5 lb.	10 - 18
7X	.004	2.5 lb.	14 - 24
8X	.003	1.0 lb.	18 - 28

The "X" designation represents .001" increments. Example: 4X is .001" larger than 5X; 6X is .001" larger than 7X, and so on.

Leader/Tippet to Hook Size Formula

This formula will help determine the size of leader or tippet material to a specific hook. Divide the hook size of the fly by 3 to get the leader or tippet size.

Fly size ÷ 3 = Leader/Tippet size.

Example: Size 12 hook ÷ 3 = 4X Leader/Tippet size.

Weight of a Fish Chart

Girth	Length 12"	13"	14"	15"	16"	17"	18"	19"	20"	21"	22"
4"	0.3	0.3									
5"	0.4	0.4	0.5	0.5							
6"	0.6	0.6	0.7	0.7	0.8	0.8					
7"	0.8	0.8	0.9	1	1.1	1.1	1.2	1.2			
8"	1	1.1	1.2	1.3	1.4	1.4	1.5	1.6	1.7	1.8	
9"	1.3	1.4	1.5	1.6	1.7	1.8	2	2	2.1	2.2	2.3
10"			1.9	2	2.1	2.2	2.4	2.5	2.6	2.8	2.9
11"					2.6	2.7	2.9	3	3.2	3.4	3.5
12"							3.4	3.6	3.8	4	4.2
13"							4	4.2	4.5	4.7	4.9
14"									5.1	5.4	5.7

	23"	24"	25"	26"	27"	28"	29"	30"	31"	32"	33"
10"	3.0	3.2	3.3								
11"	3.7	3.8	4	4.1	4.3						
12"	4.4	4.6	4.7	4.9	5.1	5.3	5.5				
13"	5.1	5.4	5.6	5.8	6	6.2	6.5	6.7	6.9		
14"	5.9	6.2	6.5	6.7	7	7.2	7.5	7.7	8	8.3	8.5
15"		7.1	7.4	7.7	8	8.3	8.6	8.9	9.2	9.5	9.8
16"		8.1	8.4	8.8	9.1	9.4	9.8	10.1	10.4	10.8	11.1
17"		9.1	9.5	9.9	10.3	10.7	11	11.4	11.8	12.2	12.6
18"		10.2	10.7	11.1	11.5	11.9	12.4	12.8	13.2	13.6	14.1
19"				12.4	12.8	13.3	13.8	14.3	14.7	15.2	15.7
20"						14.7	15.3	15.8	16.3	16.8	17.4
21"								17.4	18	18.6	19.2
22"										20.4	21

* All weights are approximated in pounds.

Weight of a Fish Formula

Species Meaurements

XX to XX=Length from
upper lip to point of tail.

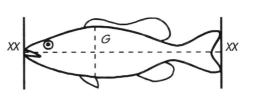

G=Girth measures around
fish at widest location.

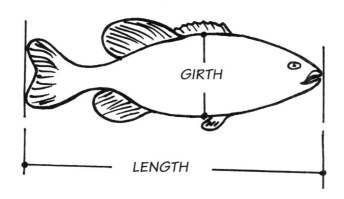

Formula to calculate approximate weight of catch

$$\frac{Length * Girth * Girth}{800} = Weight\ in\ Pounds$$

Example:

$$\frac{17" * 10" * 10"}{800} = 2.13\ pounds$$

.002" Step-Down Leader

The .002" step-down leader method says that each step down in leader material diameter will be .002," section to section. Using this method you can build a leader in either direction: butt to tippet or tippet to butt.

Example

.017"   .015"   .013"   .011"   .009"

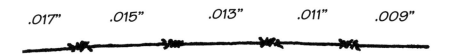

No cumbersome calculations needed.

Works well with, or when building, 25-20-20 or 60-20-20 leaders.

Works well with either freshwater or light saltwater leaders.

Note: When designing and building leaders for large bodies of fresh and salt water, the sections are in pounds.

35% Step-Down Leader

The 35% step-down leader is an effective leader that allows efficient turnover of the fly. Don't ask me why it is called the "35% step-down leader". There are many theories and if you can add more, please let me know.

Formula: Multiply the butt diameter by 2, then divide by 3 to get the next section diameter.

Example: .019" butt diameter.

1. Butt Section: .019"
2. Second Section: (.019 * 2) ÷ 3 = .0127 or .013"
3. Third Section: (.013 * 2) ÷ 3 = .0086 or .009"
4. Fourth Section: (.009 * 2) ÷ 3 = .006"
5. Fifth Section: (.006 * 2) ÷ 3 = .004"

and so on...

.019"   .013"   .009"   .006"   .004"

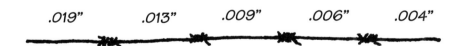

25-50-25 Leader

Consists of: 25% Butt Section
50% Mid-Section
25% Tippet Section

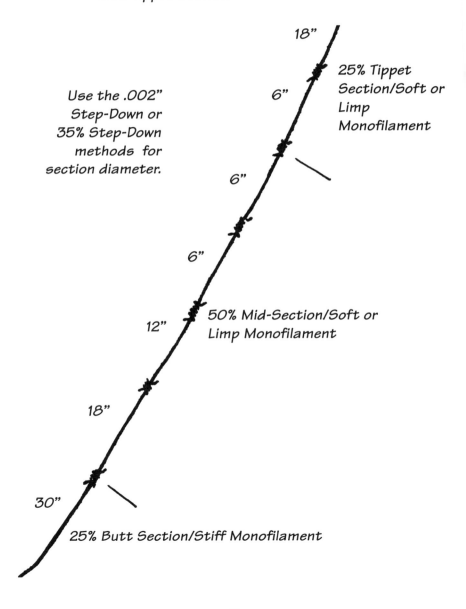

18"

25% Tippet
Section/Soft or
Limp
Monofilament

6"

Use the .002"
Step-Down or
35% Step-Down
methods for
section diameter.

6"

6"

50% Mid-Section/Soft or
Limp Monofilament

12"

18"

30"

25% Butt Section/Stiff Monofilament

60-20-20 Leader

Consists of: 60% Butt Section
20% Mid-Section
20% Tippet Section

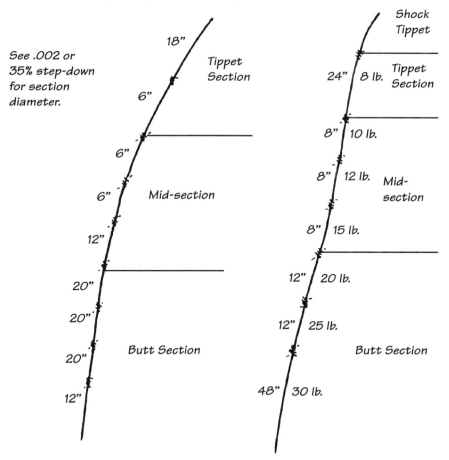

Freshwater

Adjust length as necessary.

See .002 or
35% step-down
for section
diameter.

18"

6"

Tippet
Section

6"

6"

Mid-section

12"

20"

20"

Butt Section

20"

12"

Saltwater

Try not to jump more than
five-pound-test at any one
point.

Shock
Tippet

24" 8 lb. Tippet
Section

8" 10 lb.

8" 12 lb. Mid-
section

8" 15 lb.

12" 20 lb.

12" 25 lb.

Butt Section

48" 30 lb.

IGFA Rules

The following rules apply if you wish to make the IGFA record book with a qualifying fish.

1. The class tippet must be made of a non-metallic material and either attached directly to the fly, or to a shock tippet.

2. The class tippet must measure at least 15 inches long, measured inside the connecting knots.

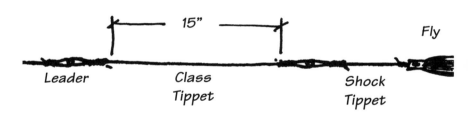

Leader   Class Tippet   Shock Tippet   Fly

3. The shock tippet cannot exceed 12 inches in length. (Shock tippet is added to class tippet and tied to the fly.)

IGFA Rules
-continued-

4. The shock tippet can be made of any type of material and there is no limit to its breaking strength.

5. The shock tippet is measured from the eye of the hook to the single strand of the class tippet and includes any knot used to connect the shock tippet to the class tippet.

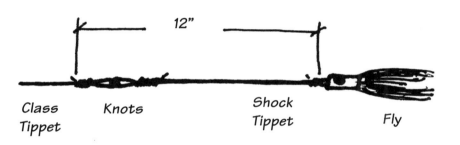

12"

Class
Tippet

Knots

Shock
Tippet

Fly

IGFA Rules
-continued-

Measurements necessary to qualify a fish with the IGFA.

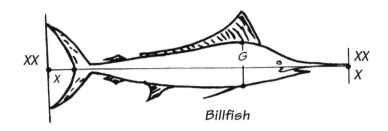

Billfish

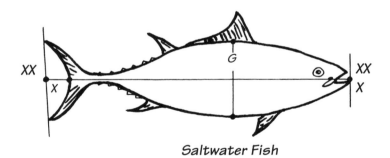

Saltwater Fish

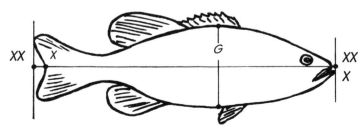

Freshwater Fish

Section Two
Knots

Knot Construction

Knot: A method of joining two lines/the joining of a line to a hook/the weakest link in a line or line system.

If a knot is not tied properly, it will fail you, no questions asked.

There are five primary steps necessary to construct a properly tied knot.

1. Lubricate the knot with saliva, water, or a lubricant prior to drawing down.

2. When drawing the knot down, do not allow the turns/wraps to overlap each other. This will cause a turn/wrap to cut into the one under it.

3. Draw the turns/wraps down slowly, evenly, and consistently. Do not jerk the knot tight.

4. After the knot is drawn down, hold both standing ends of the line, and apply one sharp jerk to set the knot.

5. Trim the tag end(s) at an angle back toward the knot. Trim the tag ends using clippers or scissors with sharp edges, do not use a flame.

Caution: Do not nick the turns/wraps. This will weaken the knot and cause failure.

Albright Knot

Used to join two lines of unequal diameters or wire to monofilament. It is also good for joining fly lines to leaders/backing.

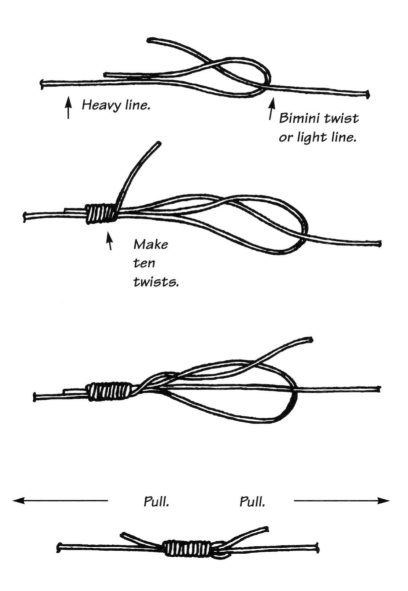

Heavy line.

Bimini twist or light line.

Make ten twists.

Pull.   Pull.

Bimini Twist Knot

The Bimini twist is a 100% knot because it acts as a shock absorber. The standard number of twists is 20. The more twists added, the more shock the Bimini can take.

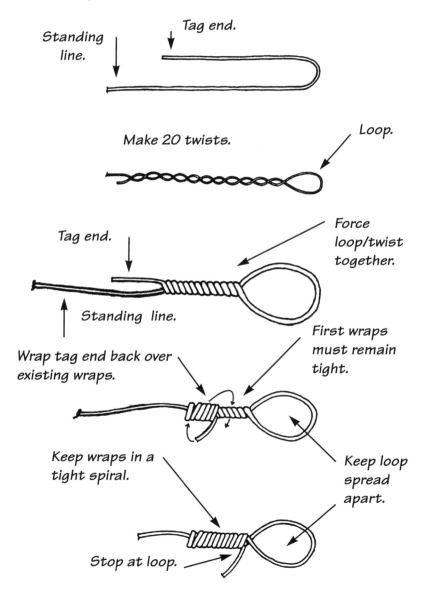

Standing line.

Tag end.

Make 20 twists.

Loop.

Force loop/twist together.

Tag end.

Standing line.

Wrap tag end back over existing wraps.

First wraps must remain tight.

Keep wraps in a tight spiral.

Keep loop spread apart.

Stop at loop.

Bimini Twist Knot
-continued-

Keep wraps tight.

Tie overhand knot as shown.

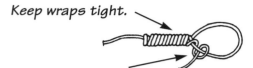

Draw overhand
knot snug and
push down
toward wraps.

Tag end.

With tag end, tie
an open overhand
knot around loop.
Leave overhand
knot open.

Loop.

Tag end.

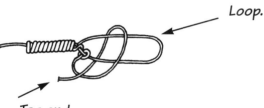

With tag end, make
two more wraps
inside overhand
knot as shown.

Loop.

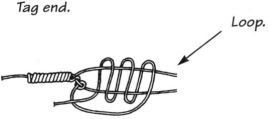

Draw overhand knot down, pull loop and tag end in opposite
directions and draw down tight.

Trim tag end.

Loop.

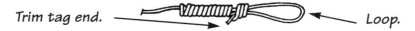

Blood Knot

One of the strongest knots for joining two lines of equal or different diameters, and for under 25-pound-test. The blood knot is close to 100 percent strong.

Form an X with the tag ends approximately 6 inches long.

Make 5 turns around the standing part with the tag ends.

Pass tag ends through center, in opposite directions.

Wet the wraps, draw them tight, and trim the tag ends.

Double Line Loop

A great, but simple, double line loop can be used when additional line strength is needed. It can be tied with mono or braided line. It has 100% knot strength.

Make loop in line.   Bring tag end back approximately 2 feet.

Standing part.

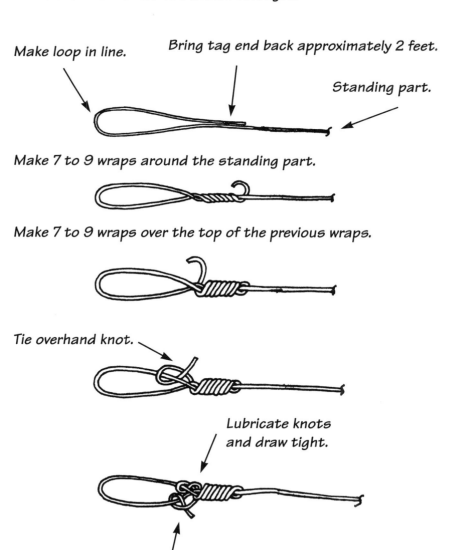

Make 7 to 9 wraps around the standing part.

Make 7 to 9 wraps over the top of the previous wraps.

Tie overhand knot.

Lubricate knots and draw tight.

Tie an overhand knot. Lubricate knot and draw tight.

Huffnagle Knot

Used to join a light fly leader tippet to a heavy monofilament (80- to 100-pound-test.)

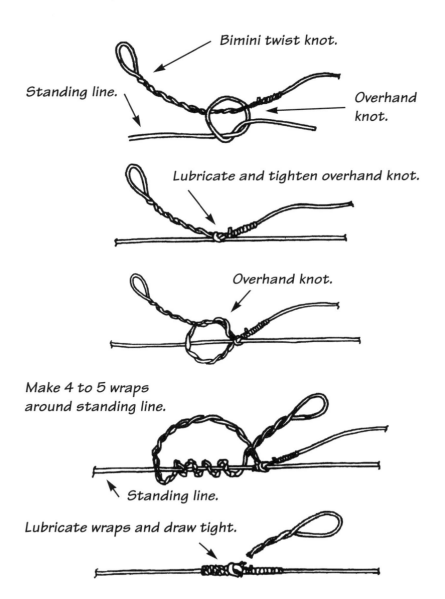

Bimini twist knot.

Standing line.

Overhand knot.

Lubricate and tighten overhand knot.

Overhand knot.

Make 4 to 5 wraps around standing line.

Standing line.

Lubricate wraps and draw tight.

Loop to Loop
-Interlocking Loops-

An easy method of connecting two lines. Ideal when changing lines in the field.

Pass loop 2 through loop 1. Then, pass the standing line of loop 1 through loop 2.

Loop 1.

Loop 2.

Note: This is the only correct way to connect loops.

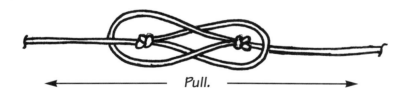

← Pull. →

This loop to loop draws tightly and evenly, and comes apart with ease.

Nail Knot

This is the fastest and easiest way to attach leader butt to a fly line, and for connecting fly line to backing.

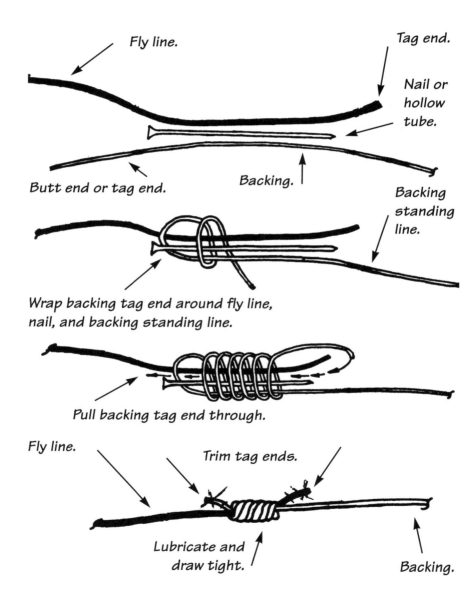

Fly line.

Tag end.

Nail or hollow tube.

Butt end or tag end.

Backing.

Backing standing line.

Wrap backing tag end around fly line, nail, and backing standing line.

Pull backing tag end through.

Fly line.

Trim tag ends.

Lubricate and draw tight.

Backing.

Perfection Loop

Ideal when tying loop to loop connections—strong and dependable.

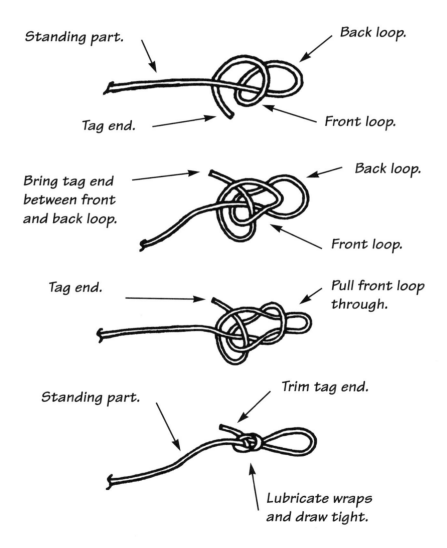

Standing part.

Back loop.

Tag end.

Front loop.

Bring tag end between front and back loop.

Back loop.

Front loop.

Tag end.

Pull front loop through.

Standing part.

Trim tag end.

Lubricate wraps and draw tight.

Surgeon's Knot

Ideal for joining lines of equal or unequal diameters, of similar or dissimilar materials. Simple and easy to tie.

Tippet.

Leader.

Tie overhand knot.

Make two more additional wraps.

Tippet.

Leader.

Draw loops tight.

Trim tag end.

Tippet.

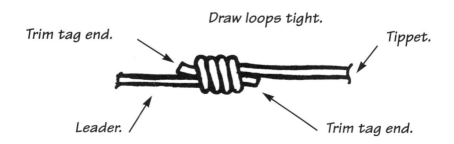

Leader.

Trim tag end.

Surgeon's Loop Knot

Use when tying two loops together, (i.e. surgeon's loop knot to Bimini twist.)

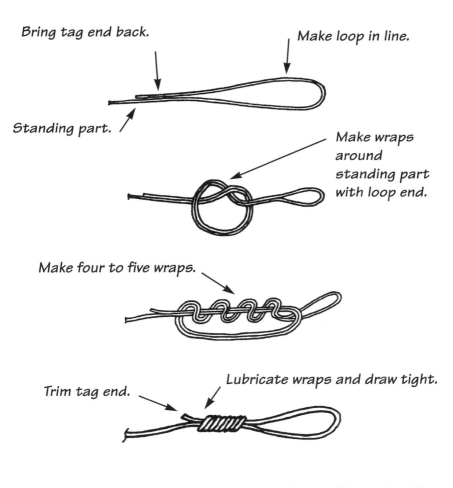

Bring tag end back.

Make loop in line.

Standing part.

Make wraps around standing part with loop end.

Make four to five wraps.

Trim tag end.

Lubricate wraps and draw tight.

Length of loop should be determined by use.

Spider Hitch

A substitute for the Bimini twist, but does not give the same shock absorption.

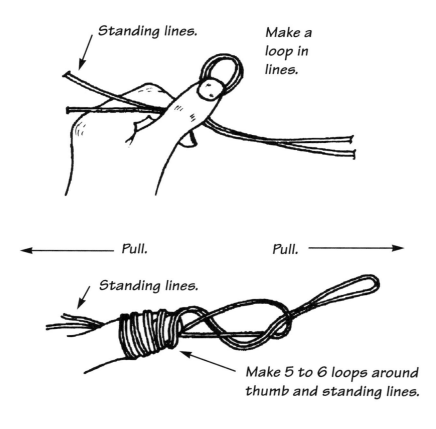

Standing lines.

Make a loop in lines.

Pull. Pull.

Standing lines.

Make 5 to 6 loops around thumb and standing lines.

Trim tag end.

Lubricate loops before drawing tight.

Section Three
Freshwater Leaders

Bunjeebutt Leader

Use the Bunjeebutt when fishing light tippets, 6X, 7X, 8X, or when break-offs occur. The Bunjeebutt acts as a shock absorber.

Bunjeebutt comes in .30mm, .60mm, and 1.00mm diameters.

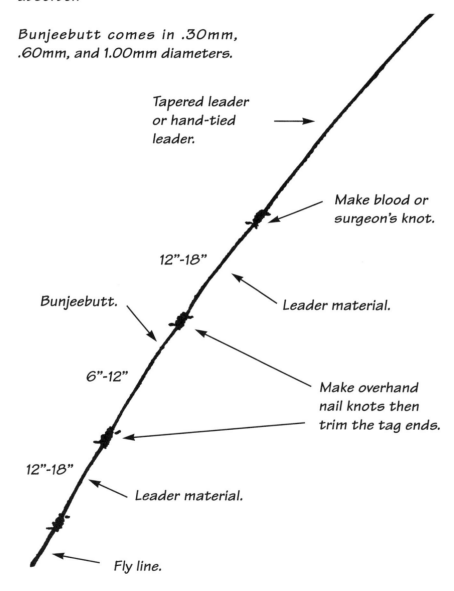

Tapered leader or hand-tied leader. →

Make blood or surgeon's knot.

12"-18"

Bunjeebutt.

Leader material.

6"-12"

Make overhand nail knots then trim the tag ends.

12"-18"

Leader material.

Fly line.

Pan Fish Leader

These leaders are used on pan fish and small bass. Idead flies: small deer hair flies, streamers, popping bugs and minnow imitations.

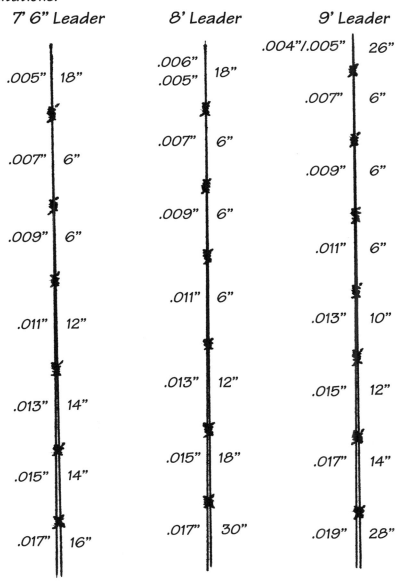

7' 6" Leader		8' Leader		9' Leader	
				.004"/.005"	26"
.005"	18"	.006"/.005"	18"		
				.007"	6"
.007"	6"	.007"	6"	.009"	6"
.009"	6"	.009"	6"	.011"	6"
.011"	12"	.011"	6"	.013"	10"
.013"	14"	.013"	12"	.015"	12"
.015"	14"	.015"	18"	.017"	14"
.017"	16"	.017"	30"	.019"	28"

Small Bass Leader

I fished this leader while with Mike V. in Tyler, TX on a windy day. I had received the leader from Joe of Kauffman, TX. The additional two sections allow the leader to unroll easier in the wind.

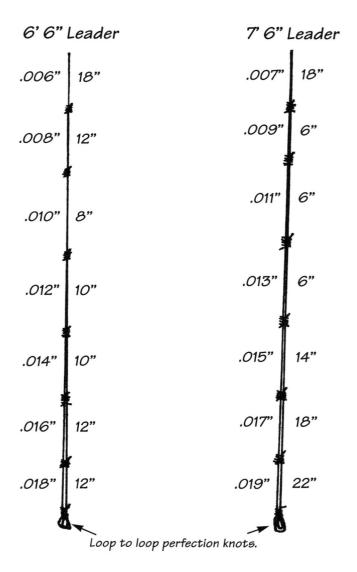

6' 6" Leader		7' 6" Leader	
.006"	18"	.007"	18"
.008"	12"	.009"	6"
.010"	8"	.011"	6"
.012"	10"	.013"	6"
.014"	10"	.015"	14"
.016"	12"	.017"	18"
.018"	12"	.019"	22"

Loop to loop perfection knots.

Large Bass Leader

I received a hand-tied leader from Bob L. on an outing in Oklahoma. I use it to fish for small to large bass, casting into holding water of 6 to 12 inches in depth.

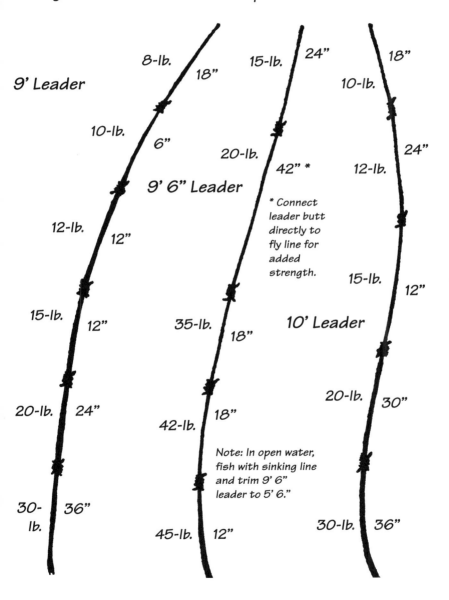

9' Leader

8-lb.   18"

10-lb.   6"

12-lb.   12"

15-lb.   12"

20-lb.   24"

30-lb.   36"

9' 6" Leader

15-lb.   24"

20-lb.   42" *

* Connect leader butt directly to fly line for added strength.

35-lb.   18"

42-lb.   18"

45-lb.   12"

Note: In open water, fish with sinking line and trim 9' 6" leader to 5' 6."

10' Leader

10-lb.   18"

12-lb.   24"

15-lb.   12"

20-lb.   30"

30-lb.   36"

Dry-Fly Leader for Flat Water

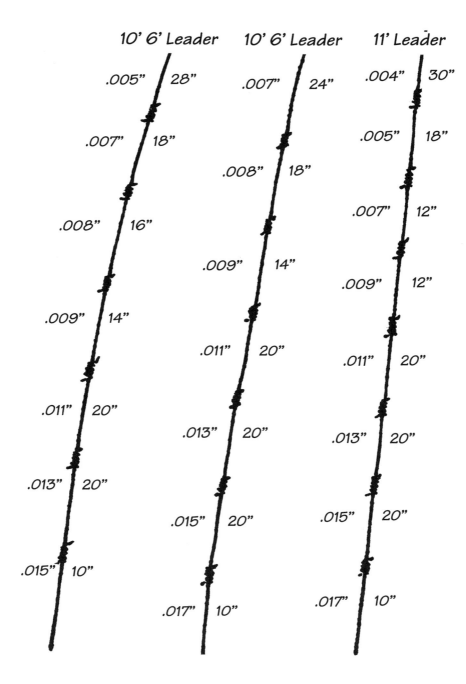

10' 6' Leader

.005" 28"

.007" 18"

.008" 16"

.009" 14"

.011" 20"

.013" 20"

.015" 10"

10' 6' Leader

.007" 24"

.008" 18"

.009" 14"

.011" 20"

.013" 20"

.015" 20"

.017" 10"

11' Leader

.004" 30"

.005" 18"

.007" 12"

.009" 12"

.011" 20"

.013" 20"

.015" 20"

.017" 10"

Dry-Fly Leaders

I use these three leaders as my general-purpose leaders. Fine-tune to meet specific conditions.

7' 6" Leader

Diameter	Length
.007"	20"
.008"	12"
.009"	10"
.011"	10"
.013"	14"
.015"	14"
.017"	10"

8' 6" Leader

Diameter	Length
.005"	18"
.007"	12"
.008"	10"
.009"	10"
.011"	12"
.013"	14"
.015"	14"
.017"	12"

10' 6" Leader

Diameter	Length
.005"	20"
.007"	18"
.008"	12"
.009"	12"
.011"	18"
.013"	18"
.015"	18"
.017"	10"

Dry-Fly Leader for Distance

These leaders are for open areas such as large rivers, lakes, ponds, etc.

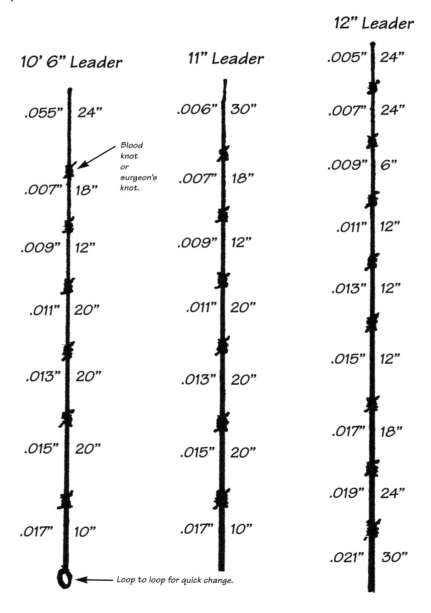

10' 6" Leader

.055"	24"
.007"	18"
.009"	12"
.011"	20"
.013"	20"
.015"	20"
.017"	10"

Blood knot or surgeon's knot.

Loop to loop for quick change.

11" Leader

.006"	30"
.007"	18"
.009"	12"
.011"	20"
.013"	20"
.015"	20"
.017"	10"

12" Leader

.005"	24"
.007"	24"
.009"	6"
.011"	12"
.013"	12"
.015"	12"
.017"	18"
.019"	24"
.021"	30"

Dry-Fly Leaders for Brush

Use these along small rivers/streams that are tree/brush-lined. These circumstances will require a shorter rod and leader.

(Leader material diameter can be changed to reduce tippet size.)

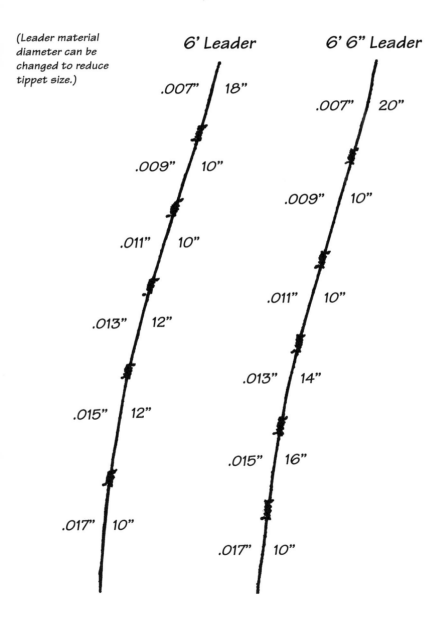

6' Leader

.007" | 18"
.009" | 10"
.011" | 10"
.013" | 12"
.015" | 12"
.017" | 10"

6' 6" Leader

.007" | 20"
.009" | 10"
.011" | 10"
.013" | 14"
.015" | 16"
.017" | 10"

Nymphing Leader

Drift nymph for trout or salmon on large rivers. This leader works best in deep waters. (i.e. San Juan River in NM, and/or large rivers in Alaska, Oregon, Washington.)

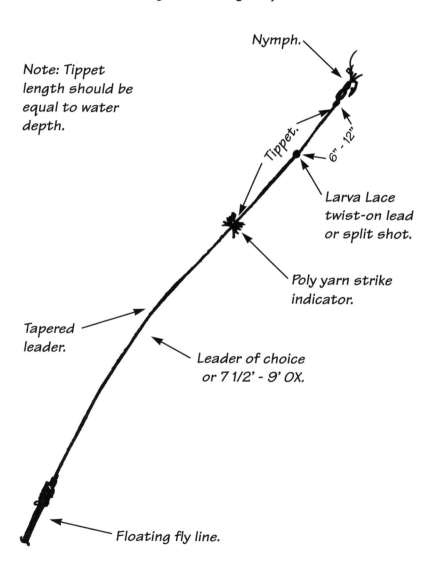

Nymph.

Note: Tippet length should be equal to water depth.

Tippet.

6" - 12"

Larva Lace twist-on lead or split shot.

Poly yarn strike indicator.

Tapered leader.

Leader of choice or 7 1/2' - 9' OX.

Floating fly line.

Nymph and Midge Leaders

Nymph—Downstream Leader

(Leader 3X + 4X Tippet
4X + 5X Tippet)

Midge/Nymph Leader

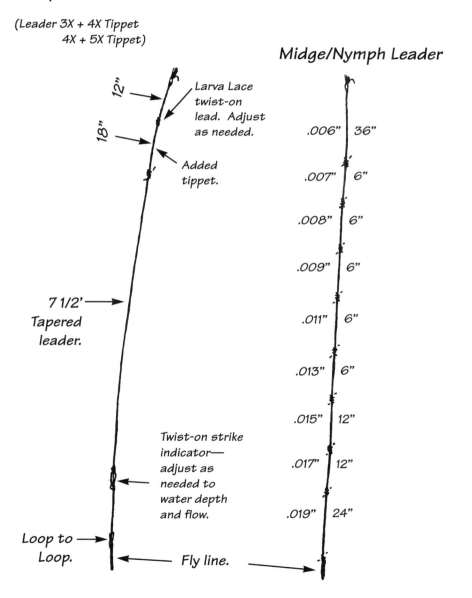

12"

18"

Larva Lace twist-on lead. Adjust as needed.

Added tippet.

7 1/2' Tapered leader.

Twist-on strike indicator—adjust as needed to water depth and flow.

Loop to Loop.

Fly line.

.006" 36"

.007" 6"

.008" 6"

.009" 6"

.011" 6"

.013" 6"

.015" 12"

.017" 12"

.019" 24"

Nymph and Wet-Fly Leaders

All-purpose leaders for a variety of conditions.

8' Leader		9' Leader		9' Leader	
				.005"	20"
		.006"	18"		
.008"	18"			.007"	6"
		.008"	10"		
.010"	10"			.009"	6"
		.010"	10"		
.012"	10"			.011"	6"
		.012"	10"		
.015"	10"			.013"	10"
		.015"	12"		
.017"	12"			.015"	12"
		.017"	18"		
.019"	18"			.017"	14"
		.019"	30"		
.021"	24"			.019"	28"

Nymph and Wet-Fly Leaders
-continued-

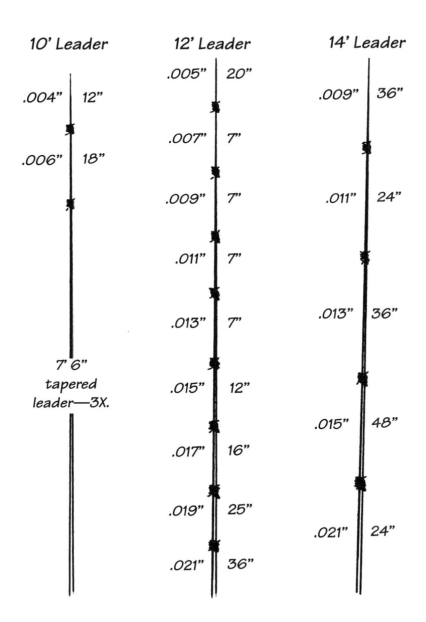

10' Leader

.004" | 12"

.006" | 18"

7' 6"
tapered
leader—3X.

12' Leader

.005" | 20"

.007" | 7"

.009" | 7"

.011" | 7"

.013" | 7"

.015" | 12"

.017" | 16"

.019" | 25"

.021" | 36"

14' Leader

.009" | 36"

.011" | 24"

.013" | 36"

.015" | 48"

.021" | 24"

Large Trout, Salmon and Steelhead Leaders

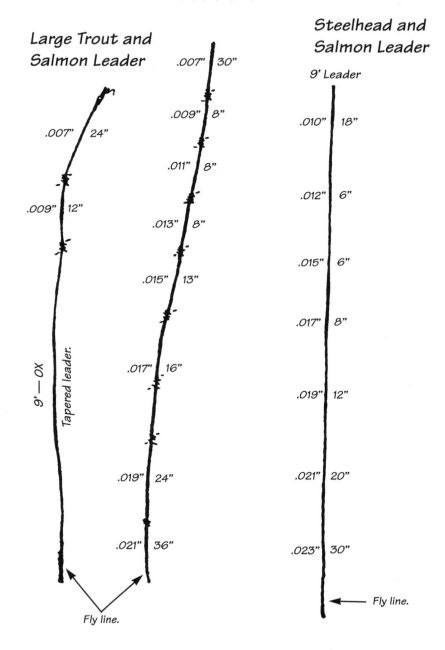

Large Trout and Salmon Leader

.007" 24"

.009" 12"

9' — OX

Tapered leader.

Fly line.

.007" 30"

.009" 8"

.011" 8"

.013" 8"

.015" 13"

.017" 16"

.019" 24"

.021" 36"

Fly line.

Steelhead and Salmon Leader

9' Leader

.010" 18"

.012" 6"

.015" 6"

.017" 8"

.019" 12"

.021" 20"

.023" 30"

Fly line.

Distance Leader

Made for distance or tournament casting—a simple but effective leader. Attach a small piece of yarn at the tippet as a reference.

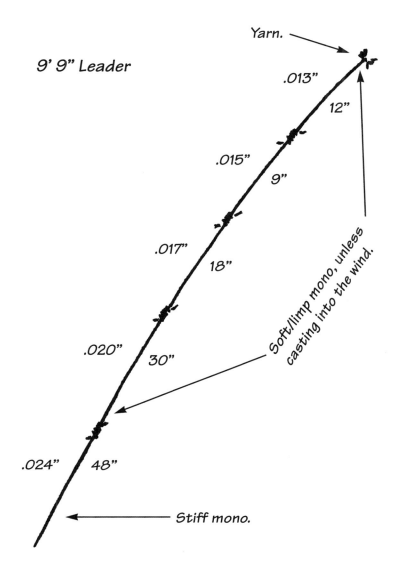

Yarn.

9' 9" Leader

.013"

12"

.015"

9"

.017"

18"

.020"

30"

Soft/limp mono, unless casting into the wind.

.024"

48"

Stiff mono.

Section Four
Saltwater Leaders

Straighten Shock Tippet

1. Heat a pan of water on the stove. Do not boil. Boiling will damage the monofilament.

2. Put the monofilament in the heated water and allow to soak for one to two minutes. This will help "unkink" the monofilament. Caution: Use tongs to remove the monofilament.

3. Pull each end of the pre-cut mono in opposite directions and allow to cool. Store the tippets in aluminum or PVC tubes and cap both ends.

Remember: Direct sunlight weakens monofilament, so always store it in a protective enclosure or in a shaded area.

Class Tippet Pre-Test

Lefty Kreh recommended this simple test to determine the breaking strength of your leader or tippet to help meet IGFA class tippet rules.

1. Take about four feet of the tippet and make a Bimini twist at both ends of the tippet material.

2. Soak this tippet in water for two hours.

3. Attach one Bimini twist to the handle of a bucket filled with water.

4. Support the bucket off the floor with the other Bimini.

5. Pour sand slowly into the bucket of water until the class tippet breaks. (Note: When the bucket hits the floor, water may splash out.)

6. Weigh the bucket and sand on a certified scale. This weight will be the exact breaking strength of the tippet. This test will help you meet the IGFA rules.

(Note: Scales used in grocery stores or meat markets are checked by state agencies and will be accurate for this pre-test.)

Shock Tippet

Large fish and sharp teeth require tippets of 80- to 120-pound test, mono and/or braided wire.

Pre-cut tippet to desired length and test prior to trip.

Store tippets in aluminum or PVC tube that is capped at one end, or both if possible.

Always inspect tippet for knicks, cracks, and abrasions.

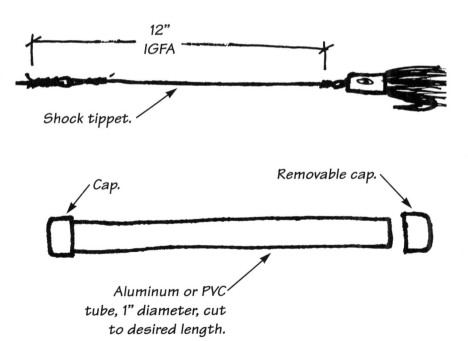

12"
IGFA

Shock tippet.

Cap.

Removable cap.

Aluminum or PVC
tube, 1" diameter, cut
to desired length.

Saltwater Fly Rig with Knots

A typical rig used for a variety of saltwater fishing. Knots may vary depending upon the application.

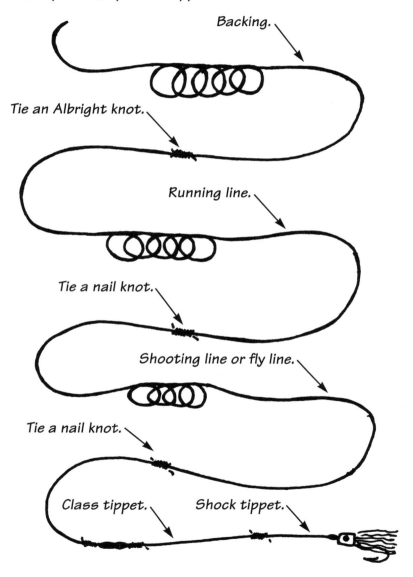

Backing.

Tie an Albright knot.

Running line.

Tie a nail knot.

Shooting line or fly line.

Tie a nail knot.

Class tippet.

Shock tippet.

Saltwater Leader Rig

A typical saltwater rig. Leader, class tippet, and shock tippet are determined by fishing conditions and species of fish being sought.

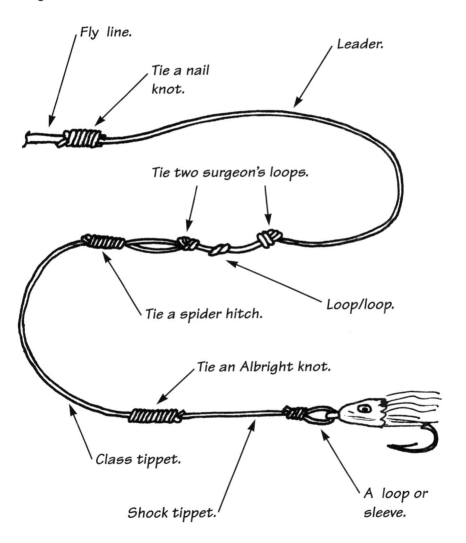

Fly line.

Tie a nail knot.

Leader.

Tie two surgeon's loops.

Tie a spider hitch.

Loop/loop.

Tie an Albright knot.

Class tippet.

Shock tippet.

A loop or sleeve.

Basic Saltwater Tapered Leader

The basic saltwater tapered leader is ideal for starting in saltwater. Test and adjust to the variety of fish you are pursuing.

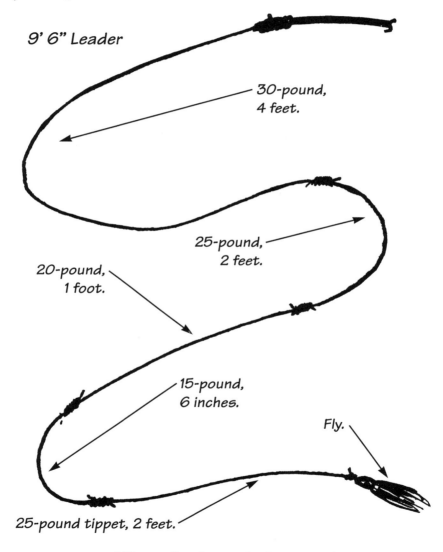

9' 6" Leader

30-pound, 4 feet.

25-pound, 2 feet.

20-pound, 1 foot.

15-pound, 6 inches.

Fly.

25-pound tippet, 2 feet.

(All mono limp for easy leader turnover.)

Deep Water Rig

This rig is ideal for use on large lake trout, bass, or light saltwater.

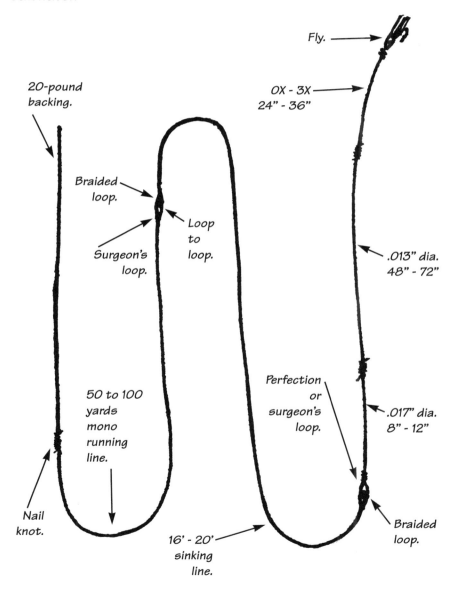

20-pound backing.

Fly.

0X - 3X
24" - 36"

Braided loop.

Loop to loop.

Surgeon's loop.

.013" dia.
48" - 72"

50 to 100 yards mono running line.

Perfection or surgeon's loop.

.017" dia.
8" - 12"

Nail knot.

16' - 20' sinking line.

Braided loop.

All-Around Saltwater Leaders

I have fished these leaders in Florida, Texas and California surf. (I added a tippet section though.) I recommend a loop to loop leader to fly line because fish size can change quickly. Leader must also be able to be changed more often because of sharp teeth and frayed tippets.

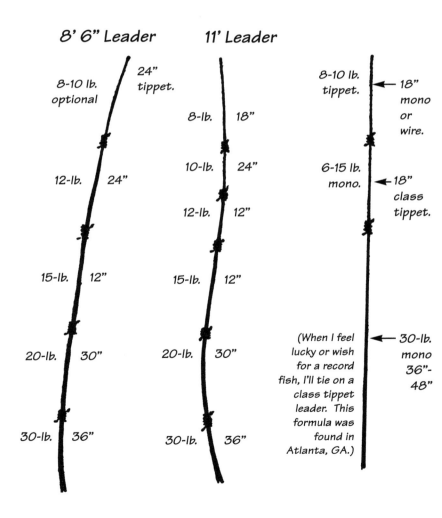

8' 6" Leader

8-10 lb. optional

24" tippet.

12-lb.   24"

15-lb.   12"

20-lb.   30"

30-lb.   36"

11' Leader

8-lb.   18"

10-lb.   24"

12-lb.   12"

15-lb.   12"

20-lb.   30"

30-lb.   36"

8-10 lb. tippet. ◄— 18" mono or wire.

6-15 lb. mono. ◄—18" class tippet.

(When I feel lucky or wish for a record fish, I'll tie on a class tippet leader. This formula was found in Atlanta, GA.)

◄— 30-lb. mono 36"-48"

Saltwater Tapered Leaders

*These leaders turn over well unless there is a very strong wind.
They are all-purpose leaders.*

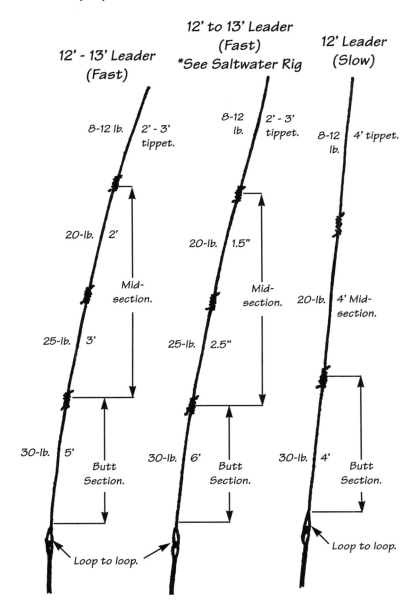

12' - 13' Leader (Fast)

8-12 lb. | 2' - 3' tippet.

20-lb. | 2' | Mid-section.

25-lb. | 3'

30-lb. | 5' | Butt Section.

Loop to loop.

12' to 13' Leader (Fast)
*See Saltwater Rig

8-12 lb. | 2' - 3' tippet.

20-lb. | 1.5" | Mid-section.

25-lb. | 2.5"

30-lb. | 6' | Butt Section.

Loop to loop.

12' Leader (Slow)

8-12 lb. | 4' tippet.

20-lb. | 4' Mid-section.

30-lb. | 4' | Butt Section.

Loop to loop.

Heavy Saltwater Leader

A customer at Bob Marriott's Fly Fishing Fair in Fullerton, CA shared this leader with me. He told me that it would work well on all large fish: tarpon, shark, amberjack, tuna, sails, etc.

9' Leader

Make a 3 1/2 turn, cinch knot to tippet.

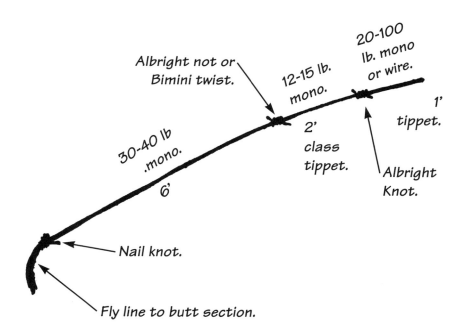

Albright not or Bimini twist.

12-15 lb. mono.

20-100 lb. mono or wire.

1' tippet.

30-40 lb .mono.

6'

2' class tippet.

Albright Knot.

Nail knot.

Fly line to butt section.

Billfish Leader

Class tippet billfish leader.

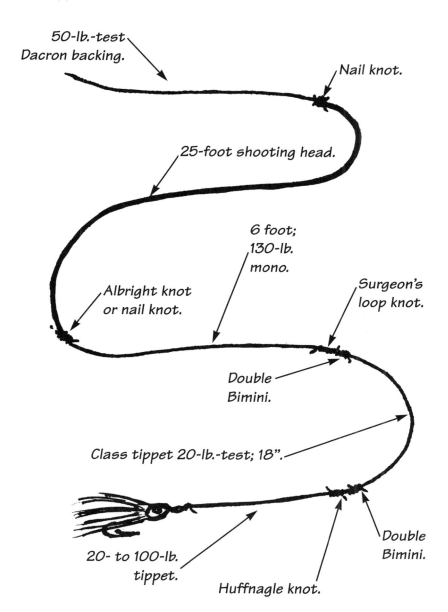

50-lb.-test Dacron backing.

Nail knot.

25-foot shooting head.

6 foot; 130-lb. mono.

Albright knot or nail knot.

Surgeon's loop knot.

Double Bimini.

Class tippet 20-lb.-test; 18".

20- to 100-lb. tippet.

Huffnagle knot.

Double Bimini.

Bonefish Leaders

This type of leader will turn over easily in windy conditions so use stiff mono in the butt section.

15' Leader, Medium-Fast

15' Leader, Fast

15' Leader, Slow

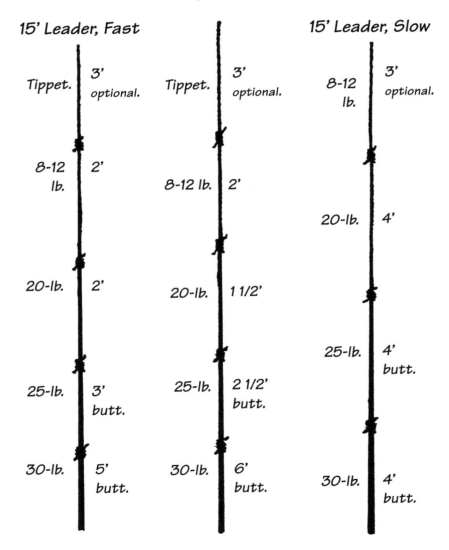

15' Leader, Fast		15' Leader, Medium-Fast		15' Leader, Slow	
Tippet.	3' optional.	Tippet.	3' optional.	8-12 lb.	3' optional.
8-12 lb.	2'	8-12 lb.	2'		
				20-lb.	4'
20-lb.	2'	20-lb.	1 1/2'		
				25-lb.	4' butt.
25-lb.	3' butt.	25-lb.	2 1/2' butt.		
30-lb.	5' butt.	30-lb.	6' butt.	30-lb.	4' butt.

Bonefish Leaders
-continued-

Three different leaders that you can use which will depend upon rod and/or wind conditions. Add additional tippet for IGFA records.

12' Slow Leader

(Added for small fish and small flies.)

30-lb.	20-lb.	8-12-lb.	6 lb.
4'	4'	4'	2'

12' Medium-Fast Leader

30-lb.	25-lb.	20-lb.	8-12-lb.
6'	2 1/2'	1 1/2'	2'

12' Fast Leader

30-lb.	25-lb.	20-lb.	8-12-lb.
5'	3'	2'	2'

Permit Leader

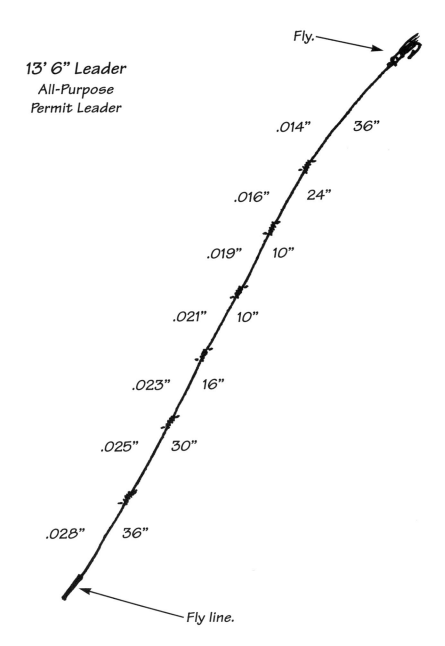

13' 6" Leader
*All-Purpose
Permit Leader*

Fly.

.014" 36"

.016" 24"

.019" 10"

.021" 10"

.023" 16"

.025" 30"

.028" 36"

Fly line.

Redfish Leader

While fishing S. Padre Island, Texas, I discovered that the fish required a soft presentation as do bonefish. This 10' 6" leader worked well. (An additional tippet can be added.)

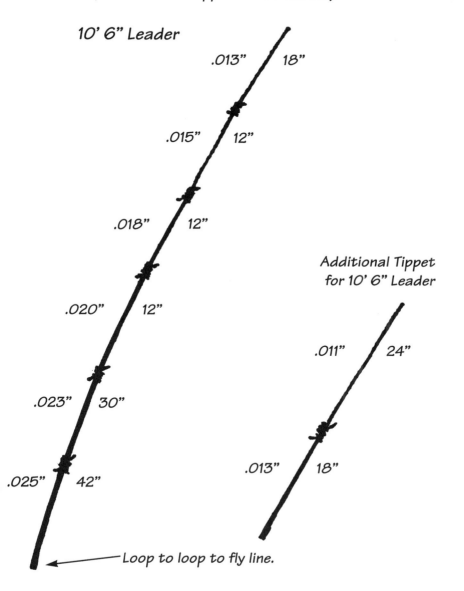

10' 6" Leader

.013"   18"

.015"   12"

.018"   12"

.020"   12"

Additional Tippet
for 10' 6" Leader

.011"   24"

.023"   30"

.013"   18"

.025"   42"

← Loop to loop to fly line.

Sailfish Leader

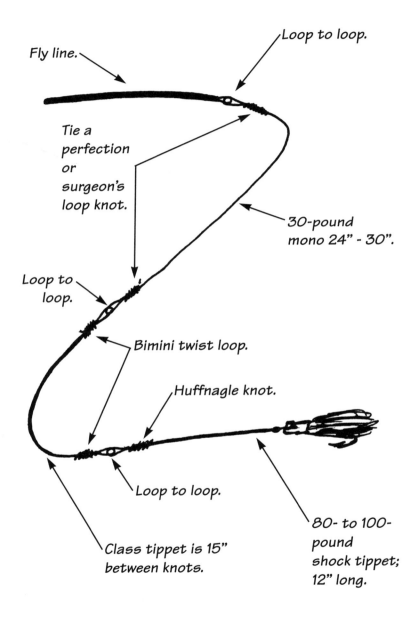

Fly line.

Loop to loop.

Tie a perfection or surgeon's loop knot.

30-pound mono 24" - 30".

Loop to loop.

Bimini twist loop.

Huffnagle knot.

Loop to loop.

Class tippet is 15" between knots.

80- to 100-pound shock tippet; 12" long.

Snook Leader

This leader is also excellent for barracuda, northern pike, and the likes. Simply change the shock leader. Note: If a shock leader is needed, use 30- to 120-pound tippet depending upon species of fish being sought.

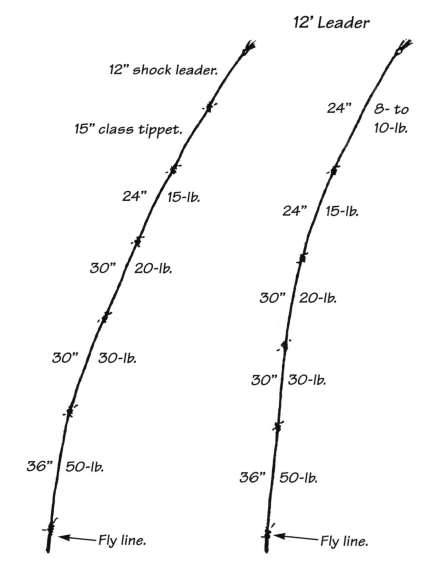

12' Leader

12" shock leader.

15" class tippet.

24" / 15-lb.

30" / 20-lb.

30" / 30-lb.

36" / 50-lb.

Fly line.

24" / 8- to 10-lb.

24" / 15-lb.

30" / 20-lb.

30" / 30-lb.

36" / 50-lb.

Fly line.

Tarpon Leader

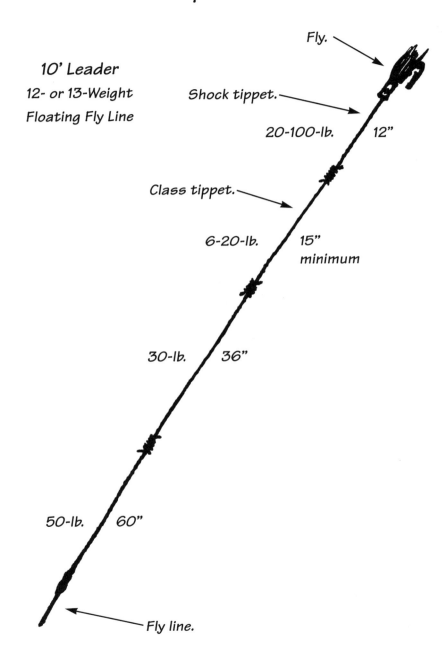

Fly.

10' Leader

12- or 13-Weight
Floating Fly Line

Shock tippet.

20-100-lb.   12"

Class tippet.

6-20-lb.   15"
minimum

30-lb.   36"

50-lb.   60"

Fly line.